Children of the World

Egypt

For a free color catalog describing Gareth Stevens' list of high-quality children's books, call 1-800-341-3569 (USA) or 1-800-461-9120 (Canada).

For their help in the preparation of *Children of the World: Egypt*, the editors gratefully thank Youssef Talaat, Egyptian Information Office, Washington, D.C.; and Amr Hassaballah, Marquette University, Milwaukee.

Library of Congress Cataloging-in-Publication Data

Komatsu, Yoshio.
    Egypt / photography by Yoshio Komatsu : edited by Julie Brown & Robert Brown.
       p. cm. — (Children of the world)
    Includes index.
    Summary: Presents the life of a young child in Egypt, describing the family life, home, food, school, religion, customs, amusements, traditions, and celebrations of the country.
    ISBN 1-55532-209-3
    1. Egypt—Social life and customs—Juvenile literature. 2. Children—Egypt—Juvenile literature. [1. Egypt—Social life and customs. 2. Family life—Egypt.] I. Brown, Julie, 1962- . II. Brown, Robert, 1961- . III. Title.
DT49.K56 1991
962—dc19
                                                       87-42578

North American edition first published in 1991 by
Gareth Stevens Children's Books
1555 North RiverCenter Drive, Suite 201
Milwaukee, Wisconsin 53212, USA

Series editor: Valerie Weber
Research editors: Scott Enk and John D. Rateliff
Map design: Sheri Gibbs

Printed in the United States of America

1 2 3 4 5 6 7 8 9 97 96 95 94 93 92 91

Children of the World
Egypt

Photography by Yoshio Komatsu   Edited by Valerie Weber,
Julie Brown, Robert Brown, and John D. Rateliff

Gareth Stevens Children's Books
MILWAUKEE

. . . a note about *Children of the World*:

The children of the world live in fishing towns, Arctic regions, and urban centers, on islands and in mountain valleys, on sheep ranches and fruit farms. This series follows one child in each country through the pattern of his or her life. Candid photographs show the children with their families, at school, at play, and in their communities. The text describes the dreams of the children and, often through their own words, tells how they see themselves and their lives.

Each book also explores events that are unique to the country in which the child lives, including festivals, religious ceremonies, and national holidays. The *Children of the World* series does more than tell about foreign countries. It introduces the children of each country and shows readers what it is like to be a child in that country.

Children of the World includes the following published and soon-to-be-published titles:

Argentina	El Salvador	Japan	Singapore
Australia	England	Jordan	South Africa
Belize	Finland	Kenya	South Korea
Bhutan	France	Malaysia	Spain
Bolivia	Greece	Mexico	Sweden
Brazil	Guatemala	Nepal	Tanzania
Burma (Myanmar)	Honduras	New Zealand	Thailand
Canada	Hong Kong	Nicaragua	Turkey
China	Hungary	Nigeria	USSR
Costa Rica	India	Panama	Vietnam
Cuba	Indonesia	Peru	West Germany
Czechoslovakia	Ireland	Philippines	Yugoslavia
Egypt	Italy	Poland	Zambia

. . . and about *Egypt*:

Ten-year-old Ahmad Asem Sakayah lives in Cairo, the capital of Egypt, land of the Nile River. His life is one of contrasts. Although he lives in the largest city in Africa, he often goes to his father's farm in the country to visit and play with friends in the fields. Like most Egyptians, he is Muslim, but unlike most other Egyptian children, he attends a Christian school. And, like many boys, he wants to grow up to be like his father, a *muhandis*, an architectural engineer.

To enhance this book's value in libraries and classrooms, comprehensive reference sections include up-to-date information about Egypt's geography, demographics, language, currency, education, culture, industry, and natural resources. *Egypt* also features a bibliography, glossaries, research projects and activities, and discussions of such subjects as Islam, the country's history, language, political system, and ethnic and religious composition.

The living conditions and experiences of children in Egypt vary according to economic, environmental, and ethnic circumstances. The reference sections help bring to life for young readers the diversity and richness of the culture and heritage of Egypt. Of particular interest are discussions of the Egyptian peoples and religions and the country's glorious past and challenging future.

CONTENTS

Ahmad lives in the Haday El Kuba district, a suburb of Cairo.

Ahmad's family's apartment.

The family standing in a field of *ful,* a type of broad bean. A cousin who ran in to join the picture is on the far right. ▶

LIVING IN EGYPT:
Ahmad, Child of the Nile

"Assalam 'aleikum." ("Peace be with you.") Ten-year-old Ahmad Asem Sakayah lives in Cairo, the capital of Egypt, land of the Nile River. The four other members of his family are his father, Asem Abdel Aziz Sakayah; his mother, Manal; and his sisters, Halah, seven, and Zaynab, four.

North America

Europe

Asia

Egypt

Africa

South America

Australia

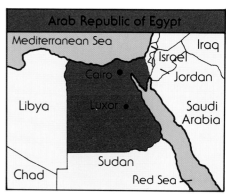

Arab Republic of Egypt

Mediterranean Sea

Iraq

Israel

Cairo

Jordan

Libya

Luxor

Saudi Arabia

Sudan

Chad

Red Sea

6

The road to Sindiyun, a typical farming village on the Nile Delta. Donkeys have pulled farmers' loads along this way for centuries.

The Family and Their Farm

In Egypt, a person's given name usually comes first, then the father's, and lastly the grandfather's, but Ahmad's last name, Sakayah, is a family name. Manal, Ahmad's mother, is a homemaker, helping to care for Ahmad and his two sisters, Halah and Zaynab. Like most Arab women, Manal's life is fully occupied by taking care of her home and family. Halah attends school near their home, but it will be another two years before Zaynab starts school. Asem, Ahmad's father, is an architectural engineer, or *muhandis* in Arabic, who graduated from the School of Architecture at Cairo University. He also has a farm in the small village of Sindiyun.

Ahmad harvests carrots for a snack.

Ahmad loves going to the farm on vacations with his family and seeing his friends there. It's an hour's drive north from Cairo on the highway that leads to Alexandria, Egypt's second largest city, located on the Mediterranean coast. The highway running through the delta is always congested with buses and cars. When trains pass on the railroad running parallel to the road, the noise is almost overwhelming.

Early ful are also good raw.

Ahmad wishes he were allowed to drive the new tractor.

While his father makes his rounds of the fields and poultry houses, checking to see if the farm has been doing well during the time the family was in Cairo, Ahmad is busy with his friends, especially Sherif, age eight, and Sherif's cousins. They can get different kinds of snacks from the fields all year round. Today, Sherif and Ahmad dig up carrots from the field, wash them with hand-pumped water from a well, and eat them in big bites.

When they get tired, they eat ful right off the plants or pick mandarin oranges from the trees. Ahmad often gets out of breath trying to keep up with the hardy village children.

Although Ahmad, like Asem, usually wears Western clothing, the traditional Egyptian clothing for older males is a one-piece, wide-skirted robe called a *galabayya*. When relaxing at home or on the farm, Ahmad's father puts on a galabayya. The hem reaches his ankles, holding the cool air around his legs, even when he walks in the intense summer sun.

In the past, most men wore the galabayya, although now Western clothes are much more common. In Sindiyun, many of the children still wear a cotton galabayya in summer and a wool one in winter.

Egyptians use the camel for cultivating fields and hauling goods. They also eat its meat.

Just a generation ago, harvested ful were packed onto the backs of camels. As the camel walked along, the bags dribbled beans. Children would hold up the hems of their galabayyas with both arms to make a basket for catching the ful. The child who collected the most earned everyone's admiration. The galabayya clearly had its uses for children as well.

Unlike many Middle Eastern women, Egyptian women do not wear a veil across their face. Traditionally, married women wear a black outer dress over a brightly colored housedress. In the villages, women often wear gold or silver necklaces, bracelets, and anklets. This jewelry is a woman's insurance against poverty if her husband dies or divorces her.

Taking honey from a beehive.

Rabbits are raised for food.

Life in the Village

Egypt is mostly desert. In the south, the Nile River snakes through the desert. But from the Cairo area in the north, the river begins to spread like a fan, forming a delta. Only 3% or 4% of the land is inhabitable, and that is mostly found in the greenbelt along the Nile or the delta fanning out downstream. The delta region was formed over the ages by accumulated fertile mud cast up by the Nile, which flooded the land yearly. Called *kemet,* black land, since ancient times, it furnishes the wealth of plant life that is Egypt's lifeline. When the Aswan High Dam was built on the Nile's southern part in 1971, it stopped these floods, making farming more predictable. Unfortunately, it also reduced the amount of rich silt carried downstream.

Sindiyun, a typical farm village, is located in Kalyobeya, one of Egypt's 26 governorates, or districts. Library records show that Sindiyun is one of the oldest villages on the delta.

Ahmad's family's farmhouse is large and grand, but most village houses are made of mud bricks dried in the sun. Their thick walls insulate against the afternoon heat. Egyptians use their flat roofs for sleeping in hot weather and store their crops there as well.

Sometimes Egyptians make pigeon houses outside their homes. They knock the bottoms off of jars and stick them together with mud from the Nile to make rather strange-looking homes. Pigeon is a popular meal in Egypt.

Besides growing vegetables and fruit at his farm, Asem also keeps bees, rabbits, and poultry. Rabbit meat is made into a soup with a vegetable called *molokheya* or cooked into crisp nuggets in butter.

Right now, Asem is constructing another poultry house. The houses must be kept at a certain temperature to help the chickens lay eggs. When Ahmad walks inside the poultry house, he feels strange in the sticky, warm air.

Ahmad and Halah like to feed the chicks.

With Sherif under the mandarin orange trees.

15

Ahmad stops next to an irrigation canal.

Canals Extend the Nile River

When Ahmad tires of playing in the village, he strolls along the canal bringing water from the Nile. Along the way, he meets mules, camels, and cars returning from work in the fields. The cars stir up clouds of dust on the dirt road, as do the briskly trotting hooves of the mules. The camels sway along gently, though, raising very little dust.

The Nile flows from two sources, one in Uganda and one in Ethiopia. Around Khartoum in Sudan, the two converge into a single vast current. Winding through the desert for 4,160 miles (6,700 km), the Nile empties into the Mediterranean Sea.

When Ahmad returns home, everyone has a snack.

Canals pulling water out of the Nile form channels all through the delta's green areas. Water is drawn from the canals by electrical pumps, human labor, or water wheels turned by cows or mules, then piped to the fields. In villages, women balance water jars on their head to carry the precious liquid back to their homes.

Also used for doing laundry and dishes, canals are definitely the water channel of daily life. Since more homes are being connected to the public water supply, however, washing clothes in the river is becoming a less frequent sight. But in Sindiyun and other villages, it is still common.

St. Fatima, a Private School

Ahmad is a student at St. Fatima, a private elementary school. The school is located in the Abbasiya district on the road between central Cairo and the new commercial district, Heliopolis. Although Ahmad is a Muslim like most other Egyptians, his school is Christian. Most children in Egypt attend Muslim public schools.

Besides religion, the differences between Muslim Egyptians and Christian Egyptians are few. The two religions have peacefully existed side by side for centuries in Egypt.

St. Fatima School goes from kindergarten through high school. The elementary and junior high schools share a building, and the high school is separate. Like all Egyptian schools, St. Fatima has a very high enrollment; the total number of students attending two years of kindergarten and nine years of elementary and junior high school is over 1,000.

St. Fatima School.

Ahmad's textbooks.

The school yard and building.

Egypt's population increases by one million people every eight to nine months, and 50% of the population is under the age of 18. The government can't train teachers or build schools fast enough to keep up with the growing number of children.

Egyptian schools are so crowded that many must divide their classes into morning and afternoon shifts to make maximum use of their classrooms. Although private schools are crowded as well, they can pay more attention to the individual child. So upper-middle-class families like Ahmad's usually send their children to private schools.

Ahmad and Mustafa in their classroom.

Ahmad is in the 5th grade, which is divided into four sections. There are 41 children in his section. Every morning at 7:10, he boards a school bus with his friend Mustafa.

When the bell rings at 7:45 a.m., all the students walk out into the school yard and line up in classes for the morning assembly. After singing the national anthem, they file into their classrooms and wait for class to begin.

Classes start at 8:00 a.m., and each period lasts 45 minutes. The four periods in the morning and four in the afternoon are broken up by a 45-minute lunch break.

The school entrance.

Although only in the 5th grade, Ahmad studies Arabic, English, French, math, science, social studies, music, and more. School is out around 3:00 p.m., but his heavy load of homework keeps him busy during the evening.

Ahmad wants to be a muhandis when he grows up, just like his father. Medicine and engineering compete for the position of most-coveted career of Egyptian boys.

After returning from school, the children relax in the living room with tea and cakes.

Education in Egypt

A college graduate in Egypt will have attended six years of elementary school, three years of junior high, three of high school, and usually five years of college. Until 1986, children were not required to attend school after 6th grade, but now they must also finish junior high school.

Schools are closed on Friday, Islam's holy day of rest, but St. Fatima has its second holiday on Sunday because it is a Christian school. After 7th grade, the second day off changes to Saturday to give children two days off in a row.

Ahmad's desk.

Arabic is read from right to left.

High school classes last 50 minutes, five minutes longer than classes in elementary and junior high school. During the Islamic month of Ramadan, when practicing Muslims fast from sunrise to sunset, school starts at 9:00, an hour later than usual.

Ahmad looks forward to St. Fatima's summer vacation, which lasts from mid-May to mid-September. His New Year's vacation lasts two weeks.

Ahmad's school bag.

▲ The library in the sporting club.

▲ Ahmad concentrates on his table-tennis game.

Ahmad's Sporting Club

Sporting clubs for the middle and upper classes are scattered all around Egypt. Besides the usual facilities like pools and basketball, volleyball, and tennis courts, sporting clubs also have libraries and cafeterias.

Ahmad's family belongs to a sporting club in the new commercial district of Nasr. Sometimes Ahmad goes there with his family, but more often he goes with other children.

Ahmad is a rather quiet boy who is not usually found in a pack of boys. Still, he prefers playing with boys to playing with Halah and Zaynab. His best friend Mustafa keeps him company going to school, playing at home, and going swimming or playing table tennis at the sporting club.

▲ A little one-on-one hoops play.

Left: The two boys mix their sports.

Muhammad Ali Mosque at the foot of Mokattam Hill. You can see its two minarets from anywhere in Cairo. ▶

Above: Muhammad Ali Mosque is one of the most beautiful mosques, or houses of worship, in the world.

Islam

Like most Egyptians, Ahmad and his family are devout followers of Islam. Followers of Islam, known as Muslims, believe in the writings and oral sayings of Muhammad, a prophet of the 7th century AD. Muslims believe that he received a series of revelations from God. Muhammad then set out to make converts within the various desert tribes to a belief in one God. In the 13 subsequent centuries, Islam has grown from a tiny sect of desert dwellers to the second largest religion in the world.

But Islam is not just a religion; it is also a way of living, for its holy book, the Koran — God's revelations to Muhammad — addresses all aspects of social, political, family, and cultural life. Beautifully written, the Koran dictates beliefs, rituals, and laws of conduct. In Egypt, as in many other Middle Eastern countries, the religion, the state, and the culture overlap, and, at times, almost blend.

Ahmad washes before entering the Muhammad Ali Mosque.

◀ Ahmad walks quietly in the mosque's great hall. Worshipers gather here on Fridays.

Right: Everyone going into the mosque must remove their shoes as a sign of respect.

27

Before entering the mosque, everyone washes their hands, feet, neck, and face to cleanse themselves.

Ahmad listens to a sermon on the Koran. ▼

Egypt's weekly holiday comes on Friday, the Islamic holy day of rest. A muezzin, or crier, calls the people to prayer five times daily, usually from a minaret. If the people are not near a mosque, they pray in the fields, in their home, or wherever they are.

28

After praying, everyone gathers in a circle to hear the sermon given by the imam.

But on Fridays, men gather at the mosque to pray together. This is called *salat el'gomah*. Muslim women normally pray at home.

Ahmad often attends salat el'gomah in Sindiyun with his father. Ahmad lines up with the village children for the prayer, which lasts about 20 solemn minutes. Then, children and adults join in a large circle to listen to the talk of the *imam*, or preacher, who led the prayer. The imam gives a sermon based on a text from the Koran and then listens as various people ask him questions about Islam. Salat el'gomah is a peaceful time.

Ahmad helps himself to macaroni at the big noon meal. Supper is a much lighter meal.

Food from the Nile

After the service, Asem invites some friends home for a lively meal. It's fun to eat with everyone, but Ahmad is dying to get outside with his friends. Bolting down his food, he dashes out the door.

Ahmad's table, naturally, is laden with foods grown on his father's farm. While Ahmad's family uses a fork and spoon to eat, most Egyptians use their right hands. They say everything tastes better that way.

Torshi is made of pickled turnips and cayenne pepper.

Cabbage mahshi.

Today's dinner is particularly splendid — *lahma-misabika*, stewed lamb and tomatoes; *ferakh*, broiled chicken; and *mahshi*, rice and spices rolled up in cabbage or grape leaves and served in soup. All of it is eaten with *aysh*, Egypt's round whole-wheat bread.

Today's menu: aysh, torshi, ferakh, macaroni, lahma-misabika, and mahshi.

31

Hammam is stuffed baked pigeon.

Shy, tea, is drunk with plenty of sugar.

Eggplant, aysh, torshi, and ful midammis.

While his mother's cooking is his favorite, Ahmad also likes the food at a restaurant near downtown Cairo. When they get a chance to go there, the family orders a set meal that includes torshi, salad, *ful midammis*, and *tahini ta'amiyya*.

Ful midammis, the typical Egyptian breakfast, is made by stewing ful in a pot until the beans get soft and then preparing them with olive oil, lemon, and salt. Ahmad scoops it up with pieces of aysh. Also eaten with aysh, tahini is sesame seeds ground into a paste and mixed with yogurt. Ta'amiyya is made by mincing raw ful, adding garlic, leeks, parsley, and coriander, and patting the mixture into balls, which are fried in oil. A popular convenience food, it can be sandwiched with vegetables between two slices of bread and carried.

◀ Dining out is a special treat for Ahmad and his sisters.

A view of Cairo from the Muhammad Ali Mosque. ▲   ▼ A view of the Nile in Cairo.

Cairo, the Largest City in Africa, and Its Markets

A population of almost 14 million makes Cairo and its suburbs not only the largest urban area in Africa but one of the largest in the world. In the past, all of Cairo's residential areas were in the greenbelts next to the Nile, but now they are spilling over into the desert. Haday El Kuba, the new district where Ahmad lives, is miles from the city center. It was created by the bursting seams of this modern metropolis.

Recently, Cairo opened the first section of its new subway, the best one in Africa. Ahmad tested it immediately. It is a little expensive but comfortable. The subway runs from the new commercial district of Heliopolis through the city center and will soon reach Helwan, a southern suburb.

Although this ancient city is becoming more modern, Cairo is as lively as ever. Buses are packed, cars follow each other in endless lines, and streets teem with people. Drivers pounding on their horns make the atmosphere even livelier.

A subway entrance (above) and turnstile (below).

The subway costs more to use than the bus. ▼

A Cairo furniture store.

A mask store and a vegetable shop.

Ahmad likes the atmosphere of the markets in Cairo and sometimes accompanies his parents when they go shopping. Modern changes have hardly affected the warm energy radiating from Suq Market, one of his favorites.

Ataba Market is near the Central Post Office. Called the "kitchen of Cairo," it is jam-packed with foods, household items, and the various spices used in Egyptian cooking. The produce is large and rich in color, thanks to plentiful sunlight and the water and rich dirt of the Nile.

Khan el Khalili, a market in an old alley, is a dark maze even during the day, reminding a foreign visitor of scenes from *The Arabian Nights*. In colorful tea shops painted with arabesque patterns, men drink shy while they discuss everything under the sun.

On Fridays, people emerge from side streets and alleys to pray in mosques. If a mosque is too crowded, in an instant, the road nearby turns into a place of worship.

Left: A spice and seed vendor.

Muslim worshipers all bow toward Mecca, the Islamic holy city in Saudi Arabia. ▶

▲ Although this is rush hour, the road between Ataba Square and Khan el Khalili Market is always busy.

An ancient ceramic hippo.

Ahmad studies a mummy case.

King Tut's treasures are on the second floor.

Treasures of Times Past

The Cairo Museum faces Tahrir (Liberation) Square, near the Nile River. Ancient artifacts are packed so tightly into the rooms that the building looks like a storehouse. The famous yellow-gold mask of King Tutankhamen is displayed in a special room on the second floor, which is always full of tourists.

Ahmad has been to the museum several times on school field trips, but the items on display seemed too old and removed

The Cairo Museum overflows with ancient artifacts.

A statue of a seated scribe.

from his day-to-day life to be important. Today, he listens closely to Asem's explanations. With all the objects excavated from tombs, burial places, and ancient villages and homes, the museum gives him a sense of ancient Egypt's history stretching endlessly back.

Ahmad's family behind Pharaohs Khufu's and Khafre's pyramids.

The famous Pyramids of Giza are another reminder of Egypt's history. Tombs of ancient pharaohs, they stand on a desert plain in a suburb of Cairo. These three are the burial places of Pharaohs Khufu, Khafre, and Nenkaure. In front of Khafre's tomb glares the Sphinx, the god-protector who is half human and half beast.

Until about ten years ago, the Pyramids and the Sphinx looked out serenely over desert and fields. But recently, the area has been built up considerably with housing, hotels, and other buildings. Unfortunately, the water used by these developments has

The Sphinx undergoes repairs.

Ahmad picnics on the car.

People wait in line to enter Khufu's pyramid.

been seeping into the ground and damaging these priceless treasures. About once a year, frightening pieces of news, like "The Sphinx's neck is about to topple off," become hot topics.

The plain is always crowded with tourists from around the world mingling with excursions of elementary and junior-high-school students from schools in Cairo and nearby areas. On holidays and during vacations, families like Ahmad's come here to picnic. It is a special pleasure to enjoy food and tea while gazing up at the sky over the vast desert and the massive Pyramids.

Egyptian Lives, a Mix of Old and New

Egypt is a land of contrasts. In bustling cities, modern buildings stand near ruins of ancient glories. Tractors till the fields where water wheels designed centuries ago still bring water. Cars share roads with donkey carts. In villages, TV antennas perch on the flat roofs of mud-brick dwellings.

Because European and North American television programs are broadcast in Egypt, young people see shows depicting lives much different from their parents', lives with luxuries not often seen in Egypt even 20 years ago. They discover that their lives do not have to be limited to the villages and farms or to the older patterns of their grandparents' lives. While Egyptian life has long been centered in farming villages, many young people now flock to the overcrowded cities to try to earn more money to buy these things.

Above: Children strap cans on donkeys to carry water from communal wells to their homes. In the background are the Colossi of Memnon.

Right: A picture of mud brick making painted on a tomb around 1480 BC.

42

But for ten-year-old Abdou, life in the village still looks pretty good. From his village across the Nile River from the town of Luxor, he walks 40 minutes to Gurna Elementary School. He is in the first shift of a school divided into two shifts. After school, he is busy drawing water and taking care of the mule and chickens.

Children play soccer in sight of the ancient Ramesseum, a temple for Ramses the Great.

Abdou's house stands on a small rocky hill on the border between the desert and the greenbelt on the west bank of the Nile. The greenbelts around these upper reaches of the Nile are thin, almost swallowed up by the immense, barren desert. Abdou can stand with one foot in lush cropland and the other in desert sterility. Even animals and insects pass quickly through the dry and uninviting desert near his village.

Bricks are still made the way they were in ancient times. These bricks will be laid for a house.

Abdou's village stands amidst the greatest monuments of a countryside steeped in the past. Even today, the area contains the most gigantic ruins, statues, and monuments in all of Egypt.

Luxor itself literally stands on its own past. In this vicinity once stood Thebes, the seat of Egyptian civilization at its peak. At its height, it was the largest city of its time. Egypt's grandest period lasted from 1570 to 1300 BC, when its capital was located in Thebes.

After Egypt lost its power and glory to foreign invaders in the 5th century BC, villagers in and near Thebes began to build their homes amidst the temples and monuments. Over centuries, village rubble and desert sand covered these ancient buildings.

It was not until the mid-18th century that they began to be uncovered and the once quiet village was transformed into a tourist haven. People from that time until now have flocked to see the greatest outdoor museum in the world.

Abdou's school friends crowd to have their picture taken.

Abdou hangs unglazed pots from the donkey's sides. His cousin Ahmed is drawing water.

Abdou can walk or ride his donkey to these marvels and to the tombs of kings, queens, and nobles. When he grows up, he wants to be a doctor, bringing modern medical techniques to his ancient village. Abdou has chosen a crucial career since a shortage of doctors and nurses plagues modern Egypt. One out of almost every ten babies dies within its first year.

Abdou, Ahmad, and other Egyptian children live with the evidence of ancient lives all around them. They see the stability of patterns of living that have lasted for hundreds of years. But they also hope to bring the benefits of more modern technologies to their changing country and to help their people prosper in the future.

Abdou's sister makes dinner.

Abdou and his father watch TV in the living room.

In the school yard of Gurna Junior High, which Abdou will attend next year. ▶

The Nile from the top of a rocky mountain on the west bank near Luxor.
Both riverbanks are green, but all the rest is barren, brown desert.

FOR YOUR INFORMATION: Egypt

Official Name: Jumhuriyaht Misr al-Arabiya
(joom-hoo-ree-YUHT MESS-er ahl-are-ahb-EE-yah)
Arab Republic of Egypt

Capital: al-Qahirah (Cairo)

History

The Oldest Country

Egypt has the longest recorded history of any country in the world. Ancient Egyptians were among the first people to learn how to grow crops, to make stone buildings, and to write. We know so much about them because of the temples and tombs they left behind, filled with carvings and paintings showing everyday life thousands of years ago.

A busy highway interchange in modern Cairo.

In prehistoric times, Egypt was divided into two kingdoms: Upper Egypt and Lower Egypt. Lower Egypt lay in the north, in the lowlands of the Nile Delta, while Upper Egypt lay upstream, in the highlands of the south. The history of Egypt really begins in about 3100 BC, when the ruler of Upper Egypt, a king named Menes, conquered Lower Egypt and united the two kingdoms into one realm. Menes became the first pharaoh of the First Dynasty, establishing his capital at Memphis in the north, near present-day Cairo. As a symbol of his united kingdom, Menes made a new double crown which combined the red crown of Lower Egypt with the white crown of Upper Egypt.

The Pharaohs

For thousands of years after this, Menes' successors ruled Egypt. The pharaohs controlled everything in Egypt — religion, government, the army, and the courts. They built great monuments to celebrate their victories, temples to worship in, and tombs in which to be buried. The famous Pyramids of Egypt were built as tombs for the pharaohs over 4,500 years ago.

The mask of Tutankhamen, one of the many treasures unearthed after the pharaoh's ancient tomb was discovered in 1922.

Under the greatest of the pharaohs, Ramses II and Thutmose III, Egypt ruled not just the Nile River and neighboring oases but all of the land that makes up present-day Israel, Jordan, Lebanon, and Syria. Thutmose's stepmother, Queen Hatshepsut, was the first woman anywhere known to have ruled a country herself. Since Egyptians were used to having kings instead of queens as their pharaohs, she sometimes wore men's clothing and a false beard to look more like their idea of a king.

Another famous pharaoh, Akhenaton, is the first ruler in history known to have worshiped only one god instead of many. His son-in-law, Tutankhamen (popularly known today as "King Tut"), became pharaoh when he was only ten years old. His tomb, discovered in 1922, was full of wonderful treasures; most stories of buried treasure and "the mummy's curse" were inspired by the tomb of King Tut.

49

Foreign Invaders

For century after century, Egypt was the wealthiest and most powerful country in the world. Eventually, though, all these riches drew wave after wave of attackers who wanted Egypt's wealth for themselves. The later pharaohs had to spend most of their time fighting off foreign invaders, like the Sea Peoples (Philistines) and the Assyrians.

In 525 BC, Persia (present-day Iran) conquered Egypt. Although the Egyptians managed to drive the Persians out 120 years later, in 332 BC, Egypt was conquered again, this time by the Greek leader Alexander the Great. Alexander founded the town of Alexandria and made Egypt a province of his empire. After Alexander died, one of his generals, Ptolemy, declared himself king. For 300 years after that, Egypt was ruled by the Greeks. The most famous of all Egypt's rulers, the great queen Cleopatra, was a descendant of Ptolemy. After she died in 30 BC, Egypt fell under the rule of the Roman Empire for the next 700 years. Egypt became known as "the breadbasket of the empire" because the rich soil of the Nile Valley produced so much wheat.

The Great Arab Empire

The most important invasion of all came in AD 639-41, when Arab followers of Muhammad, the prophet who first proclaimed the religion of Islam, conquered Egypt. While Europe was undergoing the Middle Ages (the 5th through 15th centuries AD), Egypt was part of a great empire stretching from Spain to India that was ruled by Muhammad's successors, the caliphs. After the Arab empire began to break up into several competing states several centuries later, Egypt became the capital of one of them, the Fatimid caliphate.

Under the Fatimids, who claimed descent from Muhammad through his daughter Fatima, Egypt became the most powerful and richest state in the Muslim world. The new caliphs founded Cairo as their capital, and it soon came to rival Baghdad (in modern Iraq) and Damascus (in Syria) as one of the great centers of Islam. They also replaced the old library at Alexandria by establishing the great al-Azhar University, today the oldest university in the world, in 970. Eventually the Fatimids died out and Egypt was reunited with the rest of the Muslim world by Saladin, the sultan of Egypt. During the Crusades, a series of holy wars of the 11th and 12th centuries in which European Christians invaded the Middle East and tried to drive the Muslims out, it was Saladin who organized the Muslim defense and expelled the Europeans. Although the crusaders tried repeatedly to conquer Egypt, they never succeeded.

After Saladin, however, Egypt went into decline. A slave revolt in the 13th century brought the Mamluks, a group of Turkish slaves, to power, and in 1517, the Ottoman Turks invaded and reduced Egypt to a province ruled from Istanbul.

By now, the country had been stripped of most of its wealth by centuries of invasions, but it was still one of the most fertile agricultural regions of the world, able to export huge amounts of food. In the early 19th century, the Turkish governor, an Albanian named Muhammad Ali, expelled the Turks and founded his own dynasty. The latest foreigners to seize Egypt, the British, invaded and took over in 1882. They left the sultan in office, but only as a figurehead; the real ruler of the country was a British official. Even after Egypt was declared "independent" in 1922, British troops remained in the country and British diplomats controlled Egypt's foreign policy. Once, when the king did something the British ambassador didn't like, the ambassador sent troops to storm the palace and have the king arrested!

Egypt Regains Independence

By 1952, the Egyptians had had enough. That year, a group of army officers staged a quiet revolution. They deposed King Farouk, the British puppet, and declared Egypt a republic. Unlike the British, American, French, and Russian revolutions, the Egyptian revolution was peaceful; the Free Officers, as they called themselves, came to power without any bloodshed. Colonel Gamal Abdel Nasser, their leader, forced the British to withdraw their last troops in 1956, leaving Egypt free of foreign occupation for the first time in centuries.

Nasser dreamed of making Egypt the foremost country in the Arab world. He broke off ties with Britain, the United States, and France and allied his country with the Soviet Union. With Soviet help, he built a modern army and constructed the Aswan High Dam to provide electricity and water for year-round irrigation. In 1958, he even merged Egypt with Syria as the United Arab Republic in an attempt to re-create the great Arab nation of the caliphs, but the two countries separated again after only three years.

After Nasser's death in 1970, his vice president, Anwar Sadat, another of the Free Officers, succeeded him as president. Sadat expelled the Soviets, allied Egypt with the United States, and encouraged his countrymen to think of themselves as Egyptians first and Arabs second. His greatest achievement was signing a peace treaty with Israel in 1979. Although the treaty established diplomatic relations between Egypt and Israel, it did not end the conflict between Israel and the other Arab states. After Sadat was assassinated in 1981 by extremists opposed to the Egyptian-Israeli treaty, his vice president, war hero Hosni Mubarak, became president. Mubarak's greatest task has been to renew ties with other Arab countries angered by Sadat's peace treaty, and to continue the work of modernizing Egypt. Under his leadership Egypt rejoined the Arab League and was active in the Organization of African Unity. During the Persian Gulf War of 1990-91, Egypt worked closely with Saudi Arabia to take the lead in organizing Arab resistance to Iraq's invasion of Kuwait.

Government

All Egyptian citizens who are 18 or older can vote. Voters choose members of the National Assembly, the Egyptian legislature. The National Assembly nominates a president, who is then confirmed in his post by a national election. The president is the most powerful person in Egypt. He appoints his cabinet and one or more vice presidents, and can even dissolve the National Assembly if he wants and call for new elections. The president is elected to a six-year term and can run as many times as he pleases. If the president dies in office, the vice president succeeds to the presidency until the National Assembly nominates another president.

Ancient images adorn modern Egyptian stamps.

For years Egypt was dominated by one political party: first, under Britain, the pro-independence Wafd; then Nasser's Arab Socialist Union; and then Sadat's National Democratic party. In recent years opposition parties have become legal again, and groups like the Muslim Brotherhood, which wants Egypt ruled totally by Islamic law, have been gaining strength. Despite tension between the government and these groups, Egypt has one of the most stable governments in the Middle East.

Egypt is divided into 26 districts called *governorates*, each administered by a governor appointed by the president. These governates are similar to the US states and to the provinces of Canada, except that all their power derives from the federal government. Each governate has its own regional court. Egypt also has a system of national courts, appeals courts, and the Supreme Constitutional Court in Cairo.

Egypt is a socialist country. This means that instead of taxing people to get money to run on, the government owns most businesses directly and pays people their salaries. The government owns 90% of all industries, as well as all the banks, railroads, canals, theaters, and the national airlines.

In return, the government gives its people free health care and free education, and funds huge construction projects to raise the standard of living. Egypt does allow private enterprise and foreign investment, but most of the country's wealth is state-owned.

Language

For thousands of years, the Egyptians spoke their own language, called Coptic. Coptic finally died out as an everyday language in the 19th century, but it is still used in church services by the Coptic Christians in Egypt and Ethiopia. The official language of Egypt today is Arabic. Arabic is spoken in one form or another by over 180 million people throughout the world. Three varieties of Arabic, all of them similar in vocabulary and structure, may be heard in modern Egypt. Classical Arabic is an ancient language used in the Koran, the Islamic holy book. Modern Arabic is used as the formal language for writing and in schools. Egyptian Arabic is what most Egyptians actually speak in daily life. Most educated Egyptians also speak English and French, since Britain and France were the dominant countries in Africa throughout the 19th and most of the 20th centuries.

Land

Egypt is located in the northeast corner of Africa and the extreme southwest tip of Asia. The country is the size of Texas, Oklahoma, and Arkansas combined, or a bit larger than British Columbia, covering 386,000 square miles (almost a million sq km). Its neighbors are Libya to the west, Sudan to the south, Israel and Jordan to the northeast, and, across the Red Sea to the east, Saudi Arabia.

The outstanding feature of Egypt is the Nile. The Nile is the longest river in the world, running 4,160 miles (6,700 km) from south to north. Just before the Nile runs into the Mediterranean Sea, it splits into several branches. This area is called the Nile Delta. The Nile Valley is where 99% of all Egyptians live. The soil here is some of the most fertile farmland in the world. Beautiful palm trees line the river on both sides.

The rest of Egypt is desert. The Western Desert is so flat and sandy that part of it is called the "Sea of Sand." This area is desolate except for a few oases and the small villages that have grown up around them. The Eastern Desert is an area covered with red, rocky hills, some of them reaching over 6,000 feet (1,830 m) in height. Only a few nomads and herders can make a living here. Finally, there is the Sinai Peninsula, a land bridge between Africa and Asia. The Sinai is surrounded on three sides by water: the Mediterranean Sea to the north, the Gulf of Suez to the west, and the Gulf of Aqaba to the southeast. This is the "Wilderness" in which the Hebrews are said to have wandered for 40 years, and it was here, according to the Bible, that Moses received the Ten Commandments. The Sinai was occupied by Israeli forces following the Egyptian defeat in the 1967 Six-Day War. But after the 1973 war against Israel by Egypt and Syria, the Sinai was returned to Egypt in stages until, in 1979, all of it went back to Egypt as part of the 1979 peace treaty with Israel.

EGYPT — Political and Physical

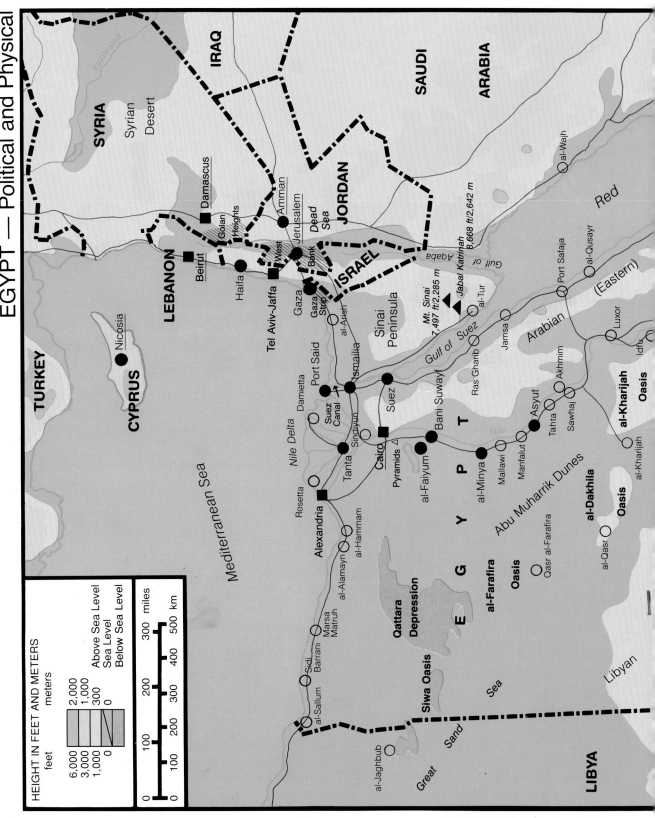

HEIGHT IN FEET AND METERS

feet	meters	
6,000	2,000	
3,000	1,000	Above Sea Level
1,000	300	Sea Level
0	0	Below Sea Level

0   100   200   300 miles

0   100   200   300   400   500 km

TURKEY

CYPRUS

Nicosia

SYRIA

Syrian
Desert

Euphrates

IRAQ

Mediterranean Sea

LEBANON

Beirut

Damascus

Golan
Heights

Haifa

Tel Aviv-Jaffa

West
Bank

Jerusalem

Amman

Dead
Sea

JORDAN

SAUDI

ARABIA

Gaza

Gaza
Strip

ISRAEL

al-Arish

Port Said

Damietta

Rosetta

Nile Delta

Suez
Canal

Ismailia

Sinai
Peninsula

Gulf of Aqaba

Jabal Katrinah
8,668 ft/2,642 m

Mt. Sinai
7,497 ft/2,285 m

al-Tur

Gulf of Suez

Ras Gharib

Jamsa

Arabian

(Eastern)

Port Safaja

al-Qusayr

Red

al-Wajh

Alexandria

al-Hammam

al-Alamayn

Marsa
Matruh

Sidi
Barrani

al-Sallum

Tanta

Sindiyun

Cairo

Pyramids

Suez

Bani Suwayf

al-Faiyum

Abu Muharrik Dunes

al-Minya

Mallawi

Manfalut

Asyut

Tahta

Sawhaj

Akhmim

Luxor

Idfu

E G Y P T

Qattara
Depression

Siwa Oasis

al-Jaghbub

Great

Sand

Sea

Libyan

al-Farafira
Oasis

Qasr al-Farafira

al-Dakhila
Oasis

al-Qasr

al-Kharijah
Oasis

al-Kharijah

Nile

LIBYA

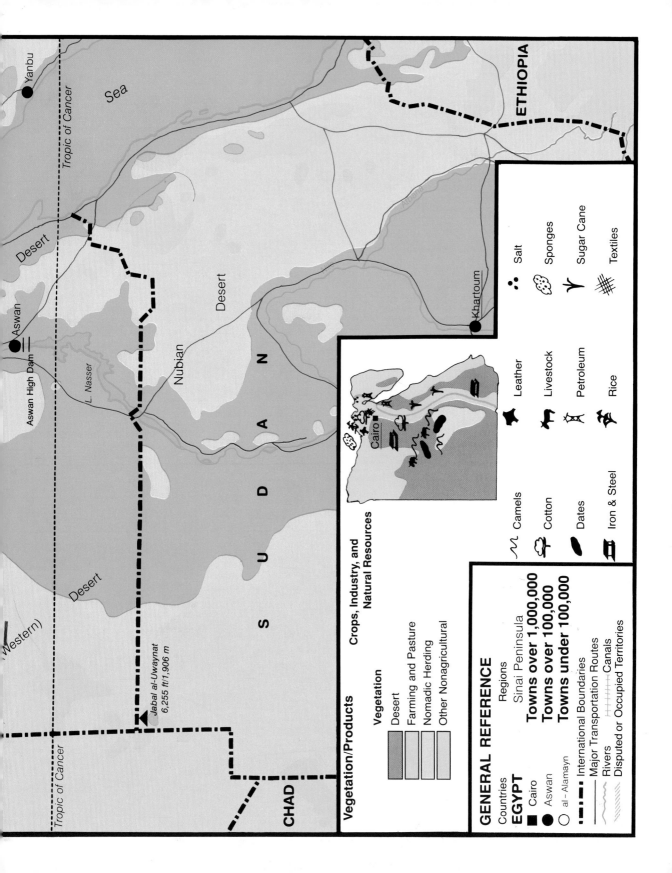

Yanbu

Sea

Tropic of Cancer

Desert

Aswan

Aswan High Dam

L. Nasser

Nubian

Desert

Desert

(Western)

Jabal al-Uwaynat
6,255 ft/1,906 m

Tropic of Cancer

CHAD

S U D A N

Khartoum

ETHIOPIA

Vegetation/Products

Crops, Industry, and
Natural Resources

Vegetation

Desert

Farming and Pasture

Nomadic Herding

Other Nonagricultural

Camels

Cotton

Dates

Iron & Steel

Leather

Livestock

Petroleum

Rice

Salt

Sponges

Sugar Cane

Textiles

Cairo

GENERAL REFERENCE

Countries
EGYPT
■ Cairo
● Aswan
○ al – Alamayn

Regions
Sinai Peninsula

■ **Towns over 1,000,000**
● **Towns over 100,000**
○ **Towns under 100,000**

International Boundaries
Major Transportation Routes
Rivers   Canals
Disputed or Occupied Territories

Climate

There is very little rain in Egypt, and that falls only along the Mediterranean coast. Egypt only has two seasons: a cool winter from November to April and a very hot summer from May to October. Since there are no trees or grass to hold in the heat, it does get cold in the desert, sometimes dropping down to freezing at night. In the summers, the daily temperature averages well over 100°F (38°C). Most Egyptians live all of their lives under the blazing sun. Only occasional sea breezes off the Mediterranean keep Egypt from being even hotter than it already is.

Agriculture

It's hard to farm without rain, but the Egyptians learned how in prehistoric times. The first canals were built by the pharaohs, along with levees and dikes to channel and hold water for irrigation. Today's farmers in Egypt use canals and reservoirs, wells, pumps, pipelines, and sprinklers to water their crops. With this technology, they can take advantage of the country's endless sunshine to grow crops year-round.

Only 4% of Egypt's land is good for farming, virtually all of it along the Nile. Unfortunately, this is also where all the people live, so as cities grow and spread out, this precious farmland is getting buried under apartment buildings and parking lots. Whereas in the past Egypt exported vast quantities of food to other nations, today the country cannot raise enough to feed all its people. Half of the food Egyptians eat has to be imported. In addition to growing rice, wheat, corn, sugarcane, and fruit, Egypt is one of the world's leading producers of cotton. Fishing is also important, with most fish coming from Lake Nasser and the Nile.

One way Egypt plans to meet its food needs is by reclaiming land from the desert. Already, a series of deep wells have turned the oases of the Western Desert into a fertile farm area now being called the "New Valley." Plans are also underway to try to re-create a prehistoric lake southwest of Cairo by diverting water from the Nile into the old lake bed. If this plan works, it will add greatly to the amount of available farmland.

Natural Resources

Egypt is one of the few countries lucky enough to be self-sufficient in meeting its energy needs. Egypt has oil, natural gas, and coal, and the Aswan High Dam provides not just water but also hydroelectric power.

Since most of Egypt is desert, wood is rare. Most houses are therefore made mainly of concrete, and some are built of mud brick, cement, or stone, just as in ancient times. With so much rock, sand, and gravel, Egypt has started a thriving cement industry. Five thousand years of civilization have used up most of the country's other natural resources, such as the famous gold mines of the pharaohs, but there are still small amounts of iron ore, phosphates, limestone, manganese, and salt.

Industry

Egypt has tried hard since the British left to become a modern, industrialized nation. In addition to the cement industry, there are also a great many textile mills that turn Egyptian cotton into cloth and clothing. Huge refineries turn out iron, steel, and aluminum products. Other factories turn petroleum by-products into chemicals, fertilizers, and plastics.

Egypt's most profitable industry, though, is tourism. Egypt is so old that the Pyramids and the Sphinx were already popular tourist attractions 2,000 years ago in Roman times. Today over a million tourists come to Egypt each year from all over the world, adding $2 billion to the Egyptian economy.

Currency

One Egyptian pound (£E) equals 100 *piasters*. Paper money comes in denominations of £1E, £5E, £10E, £20E, £50E, and £100E, as well as 5, 10, 25, and 50 piasters. There are also 5- and 10-piaster silver coins with pictures of an eagle or a sphinx on them. In 1991, £3E equaled about one US dollar.

Population and Ethnic Groups

Today about 54 million people live in Egypt. That is over twice the number of people who live in Canada, although the whole of Egypt is only slightly larger than British Columbia. Most of the country, however, is completely uninhabited: 99% of the people live in a narrow, crowded strip half the size of South Carolina running along the Mediterranean coast, Nile Delta, and Nile Valley. In some parts of Cairo, people are crowded so close together that there are 100,000 people per square mile (38,600 per sq km). About half of the population lives in cities and the other half in villages and small towns.

Nine out of ten Egyptians are Arabs, descendants of the Islamic settlers who migrated there 1,400 years ago. Descendants of the ancient Egyptians make up only about 10% of the people. Called Copts (from *qabt*, the Arabic word for "Egyptian"), they are almost all Coptic Christian and live mostly in the south. There are also a few Nubians, black Africans from the Sudan who have lived in the extreme south of Egypt since the times of the pharaohs. The few inhabitants of the Eastern Desert are mostly Berbers, a nomadic people who used to roam most of North Africa and Palestine with herds of camels and goats. Most Berbers have now adapted to village life as farmers.

Education

Despite the long tradition of learning represented by the ancient universities of Alexandria and al-Azhar (founded AD 970), before the Free Officers' revolt in 1952, 80% of all Egyptians were illiterate. Today, about 44% of the people can read and write, and this number is rising rapidly. Generally speaking, the younger you are in Egypt, the greater chance you have of knowing how to read. To try to promote education, the government requires all children to attend grade school between the ages of 6 and 12. Those who do well in school can go on to trade schools or secondary schools. A growing number, 30% of them women, make it all the way to college. All education is free in Egypt, from 1st grade through college. As in most developing countries, there is a shortage of teachers and class materials, but Egypt is working hard to train enough teachers so that everybody can have a basic education.

Religions Ancient and Modern

The ancient Egyptians worshiped many gods: Amon-Ra, the sun god; Anubis, protector of the dead; Thoth, god of knowledge; Horus, god of justice; Isis, goddess of love; Bast, goddess of cats; Osiris, god of rebirth. The afterlife was very important to them, so they built elaborate tombs to bury people in, preserving the bodies by turning them into mummies. They often buried people with things to take with them into the afterlife — a favorite chair, a mummified pet, jewelry or cosmetics, or food. We can tell a lot about what their lives were like from these tombs.

Not long after the time of Christ, Christian missionaries came to Egypt. According to tradition, the first was the apostle Mark, who is said to lie buried in St. Mark's Cathedral in Cairo, Africa's largest church. Most Egyptians converted to the new faith, and Alexandria became one of the earliest centers of Christianity. There are still many small communities of Egyptian, or Coptic, Christians today, making up about 10% of the population.

There has also been a small Jewish community in Egypt since ancient times. Before World War II, there were about 80,000 Jews, most of them living in

Alexandria. But with the founding of Israel in 1948 and the resulting bad feelings between Israel and the Arab states, most of Egypt's Jews emigrated to Israel. Today, despite the fact that Egypt and Israel have full diplomatic relations, only about 500 Jews remain in Egypt.

The Arab invaders of the 7th century introduced Islam, which would become the religion of about 90% of all Egyptians. Muslims, as followers of Islam are called, believe in the teachings of the Prophet Muhammad, as articulated in the Koran. Muhammad taught that while Abraham, Moses, and Jesus were holy men who should be honored, Islam fulfilled and surpassed all earlier prophecies. Like Christians and Jews, Muslims believe that there is only one God, whom they call, among other names, Allah. All pious Muslims pray five times a day facing Muhammad's holy city of Mecca, in present-day Saudi Arabia, and try to make a pilgrimage there at some point in their lives. Most Egyptians are Sunni Muslims, although a few are Shiite.

Egyptian Art and Architecture

The ancient Egyptians created some of the most striking buildings and beautiful art ever known. Huge temples, obelisks, statues, and tombs can be found throughout the Nile Valley. The Pyramids and the Sphinx, the most famous of all Egyptian artifacts, are an incredible 4,500 years old. The Great Pyramid of Khufu is still one of the most impressive buildings ever made. At 482 feet (147 m) high and 756 feet (230 m) long on each side, it would almost completely cover ten US football fields and reach 48 stories high.

In addition to massive buildings, the ancient Egyptians also carved wonderful lifelike statues, made delicate gold jewelry, and painted vivid scenes of daily life. This art can be seen in museums all over the world today.

Modern Egyptian art is heavily influenced by the example of the ancients, but it also draws on the heritage of Islamic architecture. Under the Fatimids, the Egyptians produced wonderful mosques, mausoleums, and palaces. They also encouraged mosaics, wall paintings, carved crystal vases, and decorated plates. The art of the Fatimids is unusual in that while most Islamic artists avoided portraying people or animals in their work, the Egyptians of the time were famous for their realistic portraits of people and everyday events, just like their ancestors of the time of the pharaohs.

Egypt also has a rich literary history. One of the earliest known books anywhere is the Book of the Dead, a collection of prayers and hymns buried with mummies to ensure their safe passage to the afterlife. Many of the stories from *The Arabian Nights* are Egyptian in origin and date from the time of the caliphs. In the 19th and 20th centuries, Egyptian writers like Tawfiq al-Hakim and Muhammad Husayn Haykal helped create modern Arabic literature. In 1988, Naguib Mahfouz won the Nobel Prize for his novels of modern Egyptian life, the first Arab writer to ever be so honored. Egypt has also had a thriving film industry for over 60 years, and Egyptian-made movies are popular all over the Arabic-speaking world.

Sports and Recreation

Most of the games children play in Egypt are popular the world over, like marbles and hide-and-seek. An Egyptian game you might not find in your home country is played with seven bricks. Children stack the seven bricks in a pile and two teams, the white team (for Upper Egypt) and the red team (for Lower Egypt), take turns knocking down the pile with a ball. Soccer is popular among older children and adults. Egyptians are also fond of sailing on the Nile in beautiful sailboats called *feluccas*.

Cairo, Crossroads of Culture

Cairo, Egypt's capital, is a city where brand-new hotels stand beside ancient pyramids and medieval Muslim mosques beside kung fu studios, video rental stores, and pizza shops. The city is especially famous for its museums, its theaters, and its many beautiful mosques. Cairo was once the largest city in all of Africa, Europe, and the Middle East, and is still one of the largest today. Fourteen million people — about one out of every four Egyptians — live in Cairo and the surrounding suburbs. The city is so crowded and housing so scarce that a quarter of a million people have taken to living in the tombs and mausoleums of Cairo's cemetery district, the "City of the Dead." Egypt's government, banking, transportation, manufacturing, education, and entertainment industries are all centered in Cairo, making it a city like no other.

Egyptians in North America

Like many other developing countries, Egypt does not have enough jobs for all its people. Therefore 3.2 million Egyptians work abroad, sending back money to their families at home. About 5,000 Egyptians come to the United States and Canada each year, a few to study in colleges and universities for useful skills to take back home, but more to settle and start a new life. The largest Egyptian communities in North America are in Chicago and New Jersey. Here and in other urban areas, immigrant Egyptians who wish to hold on to their traditional customs and religious beliefs can find mosques to pray in and grocery stores that carry a wide variety of Middle Eastern foods.

More Books about Egypt

Egyptian Hieroglyphs: For Everyone. Scott and Scott (Crowell)
An Egyptian Town. Unstead (Franklin Watts)
His Majesty, Queen Hatshepsut. Carter (Harper & Row Junior Books)
The Land and People of Egypt. Mahmoud (Harper & Row)
The Pharaohs of Ancient Egypt. Payne (Random House)
Pyramid. Macaulay (Houghton Mifflin)
Shadow Hawk. Norton (Ballantine)

Glossary of Important Terms

arabesque .... a design made up of a complicated interlocking pattern; so called from its use in Islamic Arabic art.

artifact .... any object made by humans, especially one made in ancient times.

banish .... to drive away or do away with.

illiteracy .... not being able to read or write.

modernization .... bringing something up to date; in the case of a country, adopting modern transportation, clothing, health care, education systems, and housing. An example would be Egypt's replacing caravans of camels with highways and trucks.

Muslim .... a person who follows the Islamic religion. Muslims follow the teachings of the Prophet Muhammad, as set forth in the Koran. There are two main divisions of Muslims: Sunni and Shiite.

Glossary of Useful Arabic Terms

aywa (AYE-wah) .... yes
bent (bihnt) .... girl
bokra (BUHK-rah) .... tomorrow
ezayak
   (ee-zay-AHK) .... hello; how are you?
feloos (FEH-loose) .... money
gamal (GAH-muhl) ..... camel

kwayes (KWAY-ees) .... good
lâ (LAH-ah) .... no
ma salama
   (mah sah-LAH-mah) .. good-bye
mayya (MAI-yuh) .... water
sabah elkhier
   (sah-BAH el-KHAIR) ... good morning
walad (wah-LAHD) ...... boy

Things to Do — Research Projects and Activities

Egypt and its people have played an important part in world history for the past 5,000 years and continue to do so today. When you work on the following projects, be sure to use up-to-date information whenever possible. The following guides will help you find recent articles on whatever subject you're interested in:

Readers' Guide to Periodical Literature
Children's Magazine Guide

1. Islam is the fastest-growing religion in the United States. Find out more about Muslim beliefs by visiting a local mosque, if there is one in your hometown. If there isn't, use encyclopedias, books, and newspaper and magazine articles to find out what Muslims believe and how Islam differs from other major religions like Hinduism, Judaism, and Christianity.

2. It is often said that the Nile is what makes Egypt, Egypt. Imagine you are taking a boat trip from Aswan, in southern Egypt, north to Cairo. Which cities would you pass? How would the landscape change? What birds, fish, reptiles, or other animals would you see? Write an imaginary diary covering a seven-day journey down the Nile.

3. Take a trip to the nearest large public museum and visit the Egyptian section. (If you can't go in person, check your local library for books with pictures showing life in ancient Egypt.) In what ways were the ancient Egyptians like us? How were they different? If an Egyptian from the time of the pharaohs were to visit your home, what surprises might he or she find? What things might be familiar?

4. The Egyptians were among the first people anywhere to use writing. Instead of an alphabet, they used pictures to represent words or ideas. These pictures are called hieroglyphs. Use books on hieroglyphs in your school library or articles in encyclopedias to teach yourself how to write in hieroglyphs.

5. If you would like to have an Egyptian pen pal, write to:

International Pen Friends
P.O. Box 290065
Brooklyn, NY 11229

Worldwide Pen Friends
P.O. Box 39097
Downey, CA 90241

When you write, be sure to tell them what country you want your pen pal to be from, and always include your full name, address, and age.

Index